South Africa

Mary N. Oluonye

🌿 Carolrhoda Books, Inc. / Minneapolis

Photo Acknowledgments

Photos, maps, and artworks are used courtesy of: John Erste, pp. 1, 2–3, 22–23, 24, 29, 39, 42–43; Laura Westlund, pp. 4–5, 19; South African Tourism Board, pp. 6 (left), 7 (bottom), 8 (top), 10, 18-19 (top), 21, 22 (right), 23, 33; © Trip/ L. Reemer, pp. 6–7 (top), 8 (bottom); © Jason Laure, pp. 9, 13 (bottom), 17 (bottom), 19 (bottom), 20 (bottom), 31 (bottom), 34 (left), 37, 40, 41, 42 (bottom), 42–43 (top), 44; ©Trip/ S. Harris, pp. 11, 14 (left), 15, 17 (top), 22 (left), 29, 31 (top), 32 (top), 43 (bottom); © Trip/ B. Mnguni, p. 12; © Trip/ M. Peters, p. 13 (top); © Trip/ F. Nichols, p. 14 (right); © Trip/ D. Saunders, pp. 16 (bottom), 28 (right); © Trip/ D. Butcher, pp. 20 (top), 32 (bottom), 34 (right); © Trip/ F. Torrance, p. 25; © Trip/ W. Jacobs, p. 26; © Elaine Little/ World Photo Images, pp. 27, 28 (left); © Trip/ TH-Foto Werbung, p. 30; © Trip/ J. Turco, p. 36 (top); © Trip/ D. Burrows, p. 36 (bottom); © Trip/ Hopalong Productions, p. 38; © Trip/ A. Tovy, p. 45. Cover photo of Ndebele painted wall © Trip/ M. Barlow.

Carolrhoda Books, Inc.
A division of the Lerner Publishing Group
241 First Avenue North
Minneapolis, Minnesota 55401 U.S.A.

Website address: www.lernerbooks.com

Words in **bold type** are explained in a glossary that begins on page 44.

Library of Congress Cataloging-in-Publication Data

Oluonye, Mary N.
      South Africa / by Mary N. Oluonye
            p.   cm.—(Globe-trotters club)
      Includes index.
      Summary: Examines the climate, people, languages, history, society, economy, and culture of South Africa, the largest country in southern Africa.
      ISBN 1-57505-116-8 (lib.bdg. : alk. paper)
      1. South Africa—Juvenile literature. [1. South Africa.]
I. Title II. Series: Globe-trotters club (series)
DT1719.048 1999
968—dc21   98-28175

Manufactured in the United States of America
1 2 3 4 5 6 – JR – 04 03 02 01 00 99

Contents

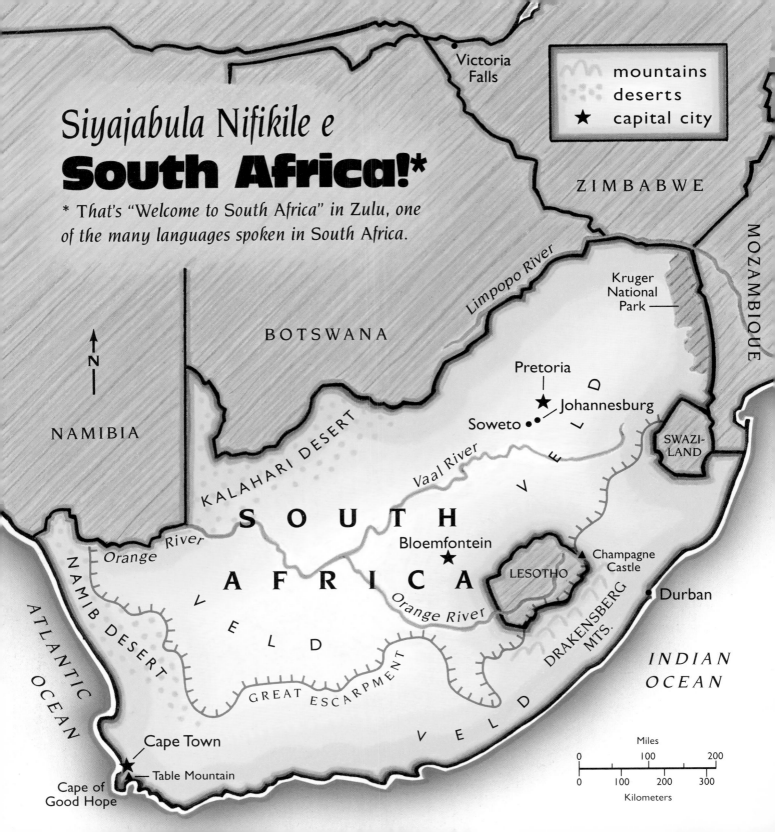

Siyajabula Nifikile e
South Africa!*

* That's "Welcome to South Africa" in Zulu, one of the many languages spoken in South Africa.

mountains
deserts
★ capital city

ZIMBABWE

MOZAMBIQUE

Victoria Falls

Limpopo River

Kruger National Park

BOTSWANA

N

NAMIBIA

KALAHARI DESERT

Vaal River

Pretoria
★ Johannesburg
Soweto

SWAZI-LAND

S O U T H

Orange   River

NAMIB DESERT

Bloemfontein
★

A F R I C A

V E L D

LESOTHO

Champagne Castle

Durban

Orange River

DRAKENSBERG MTS.

V E L D

GREAT ESCARPMENT

INDIAN OCEAN

ATLANTIC OCEAN

V E L D

Cape Town
Table Mountain

Cape of Good Hope

Miles
0   100   200
0   100   200   300
Kilometers

the mountain kingdom of Lesotho, looking as if South Africa swallowed it for lunch!

Can't find South Africa on a world map? Its name gives a clue. South Africa is located on the southernmost tip of the African **continent.** Two oceans wash most of South Africa's southern border. The Atlantic Ocean crashes against the west coast. The waves of the Indian Ocean roll onto the clean, sandy beaches in the east and the south. The country's northern neighbors are Namibia, Botswana, Zimbabwe, Mozambique, and Swaziland.

But that's not all. Take a look at the map of South Africa. See that tiny country tucked away into the eastern part of South Africa? That's

Fast Facts about South Africa

Name: Republic of South Africa
Area: 471,445 square miles
Population: 43 million
Main Landforms: Great Escarpment, Veld, Drakensberg Mountains, Namib Desert, Kalahari Desert, Cape of Good Hope, Table Mountain
Official Languages: English, Afrikaans, Ndebele, Northern Sotho, Southern Sotho, Swati, Tsonga, Tswana, Venda, Xhosa, Zulu
Highest Point: Champagne Castle (11,073 feet)
Lowest Point: Sea level
Major Rivers: Orange River, Vaal River, Limpopo River
Capital Cities: Bloemfontein, Cape Town, Pretoria
Major Cities: Johannesburg
Money Unit: Rand

Land **Ho!**

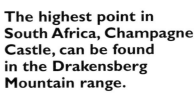

The highest point in South Africa, Champagne Castle, can be found in the Drakensberg Mountain range.

If you're looking for deserts, beaches, forests, grassy plains, and mountains, look no farther. You'll find them all in South Africa. Even though lots of water washes up against its shores, most of the South African interior is dry and sunny. In the northwestern part of the country, the Namib **Desert** creeps into South Africa from Namibia. The land here is flat and dry.

It's very different in the east, where beaches give way to thick green forests, gently rising hills, and dipping valleys. Farther inland, dramatic mountain ranges and cliffs take over. Together they make up the Great Escarpment, a rocky wall in the southeast.

Winds whip the sand of the Namib Desert into waves and dunes.

Not much grows in the parched Kalahari Desert, located in the northwestern part of the country.

The highest mountains can be found in the Drakensberg range, where some peaks rise to 11,000 feet above sea level. Drakensberg means "dragon's mountain" in Afrikaans, one of South Africa's official languages. If you fly over the mountains, you can see how the peaks got their name—they look like the sharp, spiny back of a huge dragon!

The middle part of the country is called the **veld.** That's Afrikaans for "field." Grassy plains filled with colorful wildflowers cover the veld. The land is fertile here, so it has become a favorite spot for the country's farms and national parks.

Finding **Water**

In a sunny, hot country like South Africa, water dries up fast. That would explain why lakes and rivers are few and far between. But if you look hard enough, you'll find a river here and there. Many short rivers criss-cross the land, but they are shallow and sometimes filled with sand instead of water.

Over time, the 1,300-mile-long Orange River has carved away enough rock to create Augrabies Gorge (left). **You'll find lots of waterfalls like Robeni Falls** (above) **in KwaZulu-Natal province.**

The three major rivers in South Africa are the Orange, the Vaal, and the Limpopo. The Orange River is the longest. It begins in Lesotho and flows westward across the country until it empties into the Atlantic Ocean. The Vaal River, the main branch of the Orange River, forms the border between Orange Free State province and North West province. The Limpopo River begins near the city of Johannesburg and flows into Mozambique as it makes its way to the Indian Ocean.

In KwaZulu-Natal province, short rivers race down from the craggy Drakensberg Mountains on their way to the Indian Ocean. Many streams jump from high cliffs to the flat coastal plain, creating cool waterfalls.

Lack of rain and of rivers causes lots of water shortages throughout the country. Dams, watering systems, and deep wells are used to save water and to bring it to the people. The government also asks that South Africans ration their water in times of **drought** to make sure that everyone gets their fair share.

The beach near the Cape of Good Hope looks inviting, but dip a toe in first. The Benguela Current makes the water a bit icy!

In Hot Water

Warm waters make beaches on the east coast near the city of Durban the places to play. This coast enjoys the cozy Agulhas Current that travels south from the central Indian Ocean. On the western coast, though, the waters of the Atlantic Ocean are likely to be pretty cold. That's because the chilly Benguela Current flows north from icy Antarctica. Brrrr!

The Khoisan painted animals and objects that were part of their lives on cave walls.

First **Peoples**

For thousands of years, only black people lived on the land that came to be called South Africa. These people were from the Khoisan **ethnic group.** Some of the Khoisan moved from one place to another, hunting animals and gathering berries and roots for food. Other Khoisan peoples settled down, built houses, raised animals, and hunted game. The Khoisan left hints of their daily activities through the art they drew on cave walls.

Around A.D. 300, long before any Europeans came to South Africa, a group of peoples who spoke Bantu languages, including the Zulu, arrived from lands farther north. The Bantu-speakers competed with the Khoisan for land. In time, the newcomers pushed the Khoisan south and west to the regions surrounding present-day Cape Town. Bantu-speakers settled in what came to be known as KwaZulu-Natal.

Later, in the 1600s, the Dutch East India Company arrived to set up a trade station near Cape Town. They also clashed with the Khoisan who had settled in the area. Before long, the Khoisan people had died out altogether, from battle or from diseases the Europeans had unknowingly introduced. More European settlers came and pushed into Bantu lands farther east, but the Bantu-speakers held their ground. As a result, most modern-day black South Africans are descendants of Bantu-speaking peoples.

Kraal Life

In the past, traditional Zulu homes were round buildings made of tightly woven grasses. The door was low to the ground so people had to bend down to enter. The right side of the house was for men, and the left side was for women. In the back of the house, Zulu families stored food, pots, and pans. The homes in a traditional Zulu kraal (village) were arranged in a large circle. These days few rural people live in traditional homes. Most reside in simple houses made of bricks or cement.

Long before the Dutch arrived at the Cape of Good Hope, Khoisan peoples raised cattle there.

African
Melting Pot

People of many ethnic communities call South Africa home. Black South Africans make up three-fourths of the population. But not all black South Africans have the same background. There are several ethnic groups, each with its own language and traditions. The Zulu and the Xhosa are the two largest. Other groups include the Sotho, the Tswana, the Ndebele, the Swazi, the Tsonga, and the Venda.

A mom and her son from the Kwandebele ethnic group (left) **show off their traditional garb. An Afrikaner family** (facing page) **poses for a picture at the Voortrekker Monument in Pretoria.**

About 14 percent of South Africans are white. Within the white population are English-speakers and those who speak Afrikaans, a language based on Dutch. Afrikaans-speaking whites, also called Afrikaners, came to South Africa a long time ago from Germany, France, and the Netherlands. English-speaking whites are the descendants of British, Scottish, and Irish settlers.

A group of Xhosa kids takes some time to hang out.

A small percentage of the population has Asian ancestry. Asian South Africans are the descendants of workers who were brought to South Africa from India in the 1800s to work on sugarcane plantations or in gold mines. Less than 10 percent of South Africa's population belong to a mixed ethnic group, whose members, called Coloureds, may have black, white, and Asian roots.

13

Apartheid laws forced many non-white South Africans to move from their homes (left). Signs like this one (below) were posted on trains to keep ethnic groups separated.

NET NIE-BLANKES
NON-WHITES ONLY

Days of **Apartheid**

The word apartheid means "separateness" in Afrikaans. For most of the twentieth century, the South African government strictly enforced apartheid—a system of laws designed to separate the country's ethnic groups. White South Africans controlled the government, making sure that whites got the best of everything.

The laws were very strict. People of different groups had to live in the areas assigned to them, eat in different sections of restaurants, go to different schools, and work at different types of jobs. Beaches were even **segregated,** or divided, into areas to be used only by specific ethnic groups. The majority black population was not allowed to vote, so they did not have a voice in their government.

Because apartheid favored only the white minority, this system caused a lot of violence in South Africa. Black, Asian, Coloured, and some white South Africans protested against apartheid. Countries around the world stopped trading with South Africa to show their dislike of apartheid laws.

Beginning in 1990, South Africa ended apartheid laws. In 1993 every South African citizen of voting age was allowed to vote. In 1994 Nelson Mandela, a black lawyer who had spent 27 years in prison for protesting apartheid, was elected president of South Africa.

Former president F.W. de Klerk (left) **and new president Nelson Mandela joined hands at the 1994 inauguration.**

Where **People Live**

Half of all black South Africans live at the edges of cities in neighborhoods called townships. During apartheid black people were allowed to come into the cities to work, but they weren't permitted to live in the cities. So black townships like Soweto took root. Soweto is short for South West Township. Township life is tough. The roads are bad. There are not enough homes for everyone. The houses are small and crowded together.

Since 1994 more rural homes have electricity and running water, but in the past these modern conveniences were hard to come by. It is

Check out the inside of this home in one of South Africa's townships. Since 1994 the government has worked to install plumbing and electricity in all rural and township houses.

This Soweto family (left) **has just returned from a water run. Guests enjoy a birthday party** (below) **in the backyard of a middle-class family home.**

often up to women and girls to walk long distances to fetch clean water and gather firewood for the family. Men and boys tend cattle, and everyone helps with farming.

Most Coloured and Asian South Africans are city dwellers. Cape Town has the highest population of Coloureds. A small group of rural Coloureds work in orchards and vineyards. Most Asian South Africans live in the eastern part of the country, especially around the city of Durban. Many are successful businesspeople, lawyers, and doctors.

Most white South Africans make their homes in the suburbs of Johannesburg, Cape Town, Durban, and Pretoria. They enjoy a comfortable and sometimes quite wealthy lifestyle. Many of their homes are modern, large, and roomy and are surrounded by beautiful gardens and trees.

17

South Africa has three capital cities—Cape Town, Pretoria, and Bloemfontein.

Thousands of lights make Jo'burg shine.

Big **City Life**

About half of all South Africans live in urban areas. In the major cities of South Africa—such as Johannesburg, Cape Town, and Durban—you'll find impressive high-rise buildings, shopping malls, parks, and expensive homes.

Johannesburg, sometimes called Jo'burg, is South Africa's largest city. Jo'burg sprang up in South Africa's interior in the late 1800s when diamonds were discovered nearby. These days the city is an important business center, but it also suffers from rising crime.

Many visitors say that Cape Town, South Africa's oldest city, is one of the most beautiful cities in the whole world. It faces the Atlantic Ocean and sits at the base of the famous, flat-topped Table Mountain. The slopes of this mountain rise up on both sides of the city. Sometimes low-lying clouds curl around the mountain's top. Cape Town is the home of South Africa's legislature.

18

Dear Dad,
We visited Johannesburg and Soweto today. Johannesburg is called Jo'burg by many people. We saw sparkling modern buildings, offices, and fancy restaurants. Jo'burg is a really busy city. Soweto is just the opposite. Compared to Jo'burg, Soweto is very poor. The homes are built from wood and scrap metal. In Soweto we saw President Nelson Mandela's old house.

See you soon!

South Africans like to vacation in Durban, where the weather is warm year-round. This eastern city is famous for its beautiful beaches and pounding surf. As the largest port city in the nation, Durban is also a fun place to watch ships come and go.

Table Mountain looms above the Cape Town skyline.

Getting **Around**

South African highways and roads are among the best in Africa. For people who have cars, traveling is pretty easy. But if you have to depend on public transportation, getting around in cities and towns can be complicated. People move from place to place in taxis or minibuses. Hailing a taxi is the most expensive way to go, and it's just like taking a cab or taxi in North America or

Wow, great wheels! Visitors to Durban have fun riding in a tuk tuk (above). **At the end of the day, workers** (left) **wait to hop aboard a minibus for the trip home.**

The Blue Train cruises past brightly colored vineyards in the Hex Valley.

Europe. Minibuses are the cheapest mode of transportation. But hold on to your hat—they can be dangerous. Many minibus drivers are reckless and speed along roads, sometimes going right through red lights. And it's a tight squeeze. The tiny vans are often over crowded. Tourists usually hop on a minibus called a rikki. Rikkis are more expensive to ride and less crowded than other minibuses.

If you're up for an adventure on city streets, take a ride on a tuk tuk. A what what, you say? A tuk tuk is a two-wheeled cart that's pulled by a driver. Tuk-tuk drivers usually cruise through downtown areas filled with lots of tourists.

Many people visit South Africa just to ride on the famous, luxurious, and very expensive Blue Train. People dress up for the trip, especially if they will be eating dinner on board. The train snakes through beautiful countryside as it chugs from Pretoria to Cape Town or Victoria Falls. All aboard!

An elephant (left) **grazes in Kruger National Park, while thirsty springboks** (above) **sip from a stream.**

Get **Outside!**

On the lookout for fun? Then head for South Africa's world-famous Kruger National Park in the northeastern part of the country! People who come to the park hoping to see the big five—elephants, lions, leopards, buffalo, and rhinos—aren't disappointed. Folks might also see giraffes or even the springbok antelope—South Africa's national animal—grazing among the park's grassy plains. But a trip to Kruger isn't like going to the city zoo. Visitors can actually watch the animals as they roam about in their natural habitats. Pretty wild, huh?

South Africa is home to lots of exotic plants, too. We're talking about palm trees, banana plants, smelly stinkwood trees, and tough-as-its-name ironwood trees. And what's that tree that looks as if it's been planted upside down? That's the baobab tree. According to African legend, one of the gods decided to play a joke and planted the baobab tree roots up.

But you don't have to go to a park to see these exotic trees—they grow like crazy along South Africa's eastern coast, where lots of rain falls. Trees almost disappear in the dry north where shrubs and grasses cover the desert ground. Spring rains transform South African deserts into a colorful quilt of wildflowers each year.

Take a Hike!

No really—there are lots of good places to hike in South Africa. Some hiking trails are very easy and take one or two hours to complete. But on other trails, you can expect to walk for several days. Whew! Hikers can strike out on their own, or they can join a group led by a hiking guide. Where do they sleep? Along the way, there may be huts or caves in which to crash during the night.

This thistlelike flower is the protea, one of South Africa's many exotic plants.

Zulu, Ndebele, Swati, Tsonga, Venda, Xhosa

Alphabet **Soup**

How many languages do you speak? Most South Africans can speak two or even three! And if you took a trip to South Africa, it would be possible for you to hear people speaking as many as 32 different languages and **dialects.** No kidding! When South Africa became a democracy, the government made 11 of these languages official.

Greet a South African

English	Afrikaans	Pronunciation	Zulu	Pronunciation
Hello	Hallo	Hah-low	Sakubona	sah-BOH-nah
How are you?	Hoe gaan dit?	hoo-CHAHND-it	Unjani?	oon-JAH-knee
Thank you	Dankie	DUNN-key	Ngiyabonga	ngee-yah-BONG-ah
Please	Asseblief	us-ah-BLEEF	Ngiyancenga	ngee-yan-SENG-gah
Goodbye	Totsiens	TOHT-seens	Salakahle	salla-GAHSH-leh
Yes	Ja	YAH	Yebo	YEAH-baw
No	Nee	KNEE-uh	Cha	TCHA

This road sign, which warns of hippos crossing the road, is printed in Afrikaans and English.

Afrikaans, spoken only in South Africa, is based on Dutch. But it also has words from English, German, French, Malay, Portuguese, and black South African languages. Afrikaners and Coloured South Africans use Afrikaans almost exclusively.

White South Africans of British descent speak—you guessed it—English. Many blacks also speak English, because that's the language they learn in school. During apartheid English and Afrikaans were the country's two official languages. In the 1970s, when the government tried to enforce a law requiring that Afrikaans be taught in all South African schools, black South Africans rioted in protest. To them Afrikaans was the language of **oppression.** When talking to black friends, black South Africans like to speak their own local language, such as Zulu, Ndebele, Northern Sotho, Southern Sotho, Swati, Tsonga, Tswana, Venda, or Xhosa.

Family **Time**

A South African family gathers outside its Soweto home.

Families in South Africa are like families everywhere. Parents want good jobs so they can do their best to raise and care for their children. That means having a safe place to live, enough food to eat, and the opportunity to have a good education.

South African families are close. Kids in the countryside tend to share one house with their brothers, sisters, parents, grandparents, and sometimes aunts, uncles, and cousins. In the cities, households are smaller. Children usually live with their parents, brothers, and sisters.

Keeping the family together was very difficult for black South Africans during apartheid. Families were often separated when the men left to find work in the gold mines or in cities miles and miles away. Because they were not allowed to take their families with them, the men only saw their kids two or three times a year. With the end of apartheid, black South African families have been reunited.

All in the Family

Here are the Afrikaans words for family members. Practice these terms on your own family. See if they can understand you.

grandfather	*oupa*	OH-pah
grandmother	*ouma*	OH-mah
father	*fader*	FAH-der
mother	*moeder*	MOH-der
uncle	*oom*	OO-wem
aunt	*tante*	THANT
son	*seun*	SEE-en
daughter	*dogter*	DOG-ter
brother	*broer*	BREW-er
sister	*suster*	SUS-ter

South African youngsters (above) **must wear uniforms to school. But that doesn't stop them from acting goofy once in a while! After recess, kids line up at a school in Johannesburg** (left).

School **Days**

Brrring! The bell rings at 8:00 A.M. to begin the school day. School in South Africa is a lot like school in North America. Each class is about 45 minutes long. For the first few years, students learn in the language of their ethnic group. Later they'll add English and Afrikaans to their course list. All South African kids are required to study science, geography, math, religion, and home economics. At 2:00 P.M., another bell rings. School's out!

South African kids start first grade when they are seven years old and continue their studies for 12 years. Sound familiar? After second grade, though, things change. Classes are called standards, for example.

Instead of saying that they are in third grade, kids say they are in standard one.

At the end of standard five, students go on to five more years of high school. After completing the last year of high school, kids take a big and very important set of exams. Colleges and universities look at the results of these tests to decide who to admit to their schools. What a nail-biter!

Catching Up

One of the lasting and negative aspects of apartheid were the years of unequal education. Under apartheid the old government spent a lot more money on educating white South African children than it did on educating non-white South African children. These days schools are trying to catch up, but it's not easy. Aside from the shortage of schools, especially in black areas, many schools in rural areas don't have enough teachers, books, or equipment. Improving the quality of education for all South African children is one of the new government's top jobs.

Conditions have improved a bit for Soweto students since apartheid's end. There are fewer students per classroom, more books, and trained teachers.

Religious **Mix**

Most Afrikaners attend Dutch Reformed churches like this one in Western Cape province.

 South Africa has many traditional African religious shrines. You'll also find Christian churches, Islamic mosques (houses of prayer), Jewish synagogues, and Hindu shrines and temples.

Traditional African religion has been around the longest. Followers of this religion believe in a Supreme Being who created the world. But spirits, especially those of **ancestors,** are very important. Believers feel that the ancestor spirits guide them every day. If the ancestors are happy, they will bring good luck. But if the ancestors are unhappy, bad luck may be around the corner.

Some black South Africans practice only traditional African religion, but most combine traditional beliefs with Christian beliefs. In the 1600s, Dutch settlers brought Christianity to South

Africa. As a result, most South Africans are Christians who belong to the Dutch Reformed Church.

Asian descendants introduced Islam and Hinduism into the country's religious mix. Most Asian South Africans are Hindus, followers of a faith that originated in India. In the 1800s, Jewish people from Britain, the Netherlands, and Germany settled in South Africa and introduced Judaism.

Those who practice traditional African religions may visit a *dinkata* (traditional healer) (above) when they are feeling ill. This dinkata is stocking up on herbs at the market. Church-going folks in Cape Town (right) sing hymns at a Sunday service.

Time to **Party!**

Put on your party hat! With so many religions, South Africans have lots to celebrate. Christians in South Africa go all out at Christmas. On Christmas Eve, South African kids leave their

Neon Christmas decorations brighten the streets of Jo'burg during the holiday season.

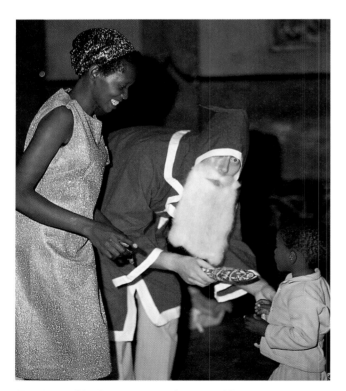

Father Christmas delivers gifts on Christmas Day in South Africa.

pillows at the foot of their beds. During the night, Father Christmas sneaks in and fills the pillowcases with goodies. What fun!

South African Jews celebrate the Jewish New Year, called Rosh Hashanah, in September or October. As part of the celebration, kids dip apples into honey and then pop the tasty treats into their mouths. The honey represents the hope for a sweet new year.

All South Africans get together to celebrate the Day of Reconciliation on December 16. During apartheid this holiday was called the Day of the Vow, a day set aside to mark a deadly battle between Afrikaners and Zulus in the late 1800s. These days, instead of remembering a tragic part of their history, South Africans use the day to celebrate working together as a nation.

Grahamstown Festival

South Africa holds many festivals throughout the year, but none is bigger or more popular than the Grahamstown Festival. In July more than 70,000 people flock to Grahamstown in Cape province to take part. Roughly 600 events and programs show off South Africa's African, Asian, and European cultural heritage.

The arts festival completely takes over the city. Posters announcing festival events are plastered everywhere, and costumed performers stroll through the streets. Artists sell their work at booths. People gather around to listen to writers and poets read out loud. Traditional, ballet, and Indian dancers entertain audiences. Music lovers have all kinds of music to listen to and enjoy.

Mmmmm...Food!

Fire up the *braai!* **Afrikaners love to grill** (left). **At this event, grillers can win prizes if their fixings taste better than the rest. Check out this steaming plate of mealies topped with gravy and a little bit of meat** (above).

Ready, set, eat! In South Africa, you'll find plenty of yummy meat, seafood, fruits, and vegetables to munch on. And, thanks to the many cultures of South Africa, there is no one single South African dish.

If you like corn, you'll get a kick out of traditional African cooking. Corn is cooked into a smooth porridge—also known as mealies—and eaten with a delicious stew made from vegetables, meat, and spices. The best part about traditional African cooking is that it's super easy—just throw all of the ingredients into a pot and mix.

Recipes brought to South Africa from Germany and the Netherlands are an important part of Afrikaner cooking. Fish and meats—like homemade *boerwors* (spicy sausages) and steak—are cooked over an open fire on a grill called a *braai*. Afrikaners like grilled ostrich, lamb, and antelope, too. But don't forget to eat something green! An Afrikaner meal isn't complete without vegetables.

Keep a glass of water nearby when you dig into Indian meats and vegetable stews—most are hot and spicy. Mouth-watering curries, fish, roasted meats, and vegetables are smothered in Asian spices.

In the mood for fast food? Instead of a hamburger, try bunny chow. A popular Asian South African fast food, bunny chow begins with a loaf of bread cut in half. Its middle is scooped out and stuffed with curried beans, chicken, fish, or vegetables. Sounds tasty!

Coconut Barfi: A Coconut Treat

You will need:
1 cup milk
2 tablespoons of margarine or vegetable oil
2 cups sugar
1 cup shredded coconut

1. Use the margarine or vegetable oil to lightly grease the cookie sheet.
2. Ask an adult to help you add the milk and margarine to a large saucepan. Bring to a boil.
3. Turn the heat down a little. While the liquid is simmering, stir in the sugar and coconut.
4. Stir for about seven minutes until the mixture becomes thick.
5. If you would like, add a few drops of food coloring.
6. Remove the mixture from the heat and carefully pour it into the greased cookie sheet.
7. Let cool. When it is cold, cut into squares and enjoy!

Art **Smart**

The oldest works of art in South Africa date back tens of thousands of years ago to the Stone Age. That's old! In mountain caves, Khoisan people recorded scenes from their everyday lives in paintings. These pictures of people, animals, hunting, and battles are also known as rock art. Each year tourists take guided tours of caves near the Drakensberg Mountains to get a close-up look at the

How about wearing one of these masks (above) **for Halloween? Wooden masks, grass baskets, and beaded jewelry are standard fare at the market in Durban. Some rock art was etched onto boulders. Item 83 is on display at the Museum of Rock Art in Johannesburg** (left).

ancient rock paintings. Can't make the trip? Rock art is also on display in several art galleries and museums around the country.

But you don't have to look in a cave to find art in South Africa—it's all over the place. Zulu women weave baskets of different shapes and sizes from grasses or other plant parts. The baskets are decorative, but they are also useful. Some baskets are woven so tightly that you can actually fill them with water and they won't leak a single drop! Craftspeople also weave grasses into simple sleeping mats.

Ever make a puppet? There's a puppet museum in Pretoria. Every Saturday morning, it's time for children's theater. Children and their parents learn how to create and handle puppets. Sounds like fun!

A Blast from the Past

Many South African families and tourists visit African cultural villages. Guests can stay in traditional African homes and learn crafts from the past. They may learn how grasses, herbs, roots, and tree bark can help cure certain illnesses. Other activities include how to weave baskets, how to make clay pots, or how to design beaded jewelry. And have you ever participated in an African rain ceremony or joined in a traditional celebration dance? You can do both at an African cultural village. No kidding!

A teacher entertains South African kids with a picture book.

Tell a **Story**

South African children love to listen to stories. The tales are fun, but many times they teach a lesson, too. Kids learn about their country's history, their ethnic group's culture, and their family's values.

Beverly Naidoo, a South African-born writer, has written several books for children. Two of her works—*Journey to Johannesburg: A South African Story* and *Chain of Fire*—describe how apartheid affected the lives of South African kids. Naidoo's book *No Turning Back* tells the story of young black South Africans living on the streets after the end of apartheid.

Another South African children's story wasn't told in a book but by actors on stages all over the world. Kids delight in watching *Sarafina!*, a musical written by Mbondgeni Ngema, a South African playwright. The play acts out the events of the Soweto Uprising of 1976, when thousands of people clashed with police.

The cast of the play, made up of black South African children, traveled to many countries. The play was so successful that it was later made into a movie starring Whoopi Goldberg.

The Maiden of the River

Long ago there was a father who had two daughters, Nomkhosi and Somate. The father loved Somate so much that there was no love left over for Nomkhosi. But Somate loved her sister and that made the father jealous.

One day he took Nomkhosi to the river and threw her in to drown. But the river guardian, a python named Monya, gently wrapped his giant coils around Nomkhosi and hypnotized her with his eyes. In the deep water, Nomkhosi became a river dweller. The fish, the crabs, and even the mean crocodiles became her friends.

Months later Somate went down to the river and saw her lost sister. Somate begged Nomkhosi to come home, but Nomkhosi was happy where she was. Somate kept it secret for a while, but one day she was so sad she told her father. To please his favorite daughter, the father went to the river and ordered Nomkhosi to return home with them.

When Monya found out, he commanded the river to rise high into bigger and bigger waves. The waves crashed ashore with Monya riding the crest. Monya entered Nomkhosi's house and carried her back into the river. To this day, the beautiful maiden lives happily with her friends in the river.

Gum boot dancing is an energetic, foot-stomping, hand-clapping, all-male jig that began on sugarcane plantations and in gold mines. Yee haw!

Musical **Notes**

Music lovers have a blast in South Africa. And they have lots of different styles to choose from! Jazz is popular all over the country. Cape Jazz is jazz combined with Asian, Spanish, and African rhythms.

You may have heard of Ladysmith Black Mombaza, a South African musical group that has worked with Paul Simon, Dolly Parton, and Bonnie Raitt. The group sings *isicathamiya*—traditional music that developed in the gold mines of South Africa. Most of the time, the group sings "a cappella" (without the help of musical instruments). Ladysmith Black Mombaza's Zulu songs are about peace and love. The group sure gets around. They provided the entertainment when Nelson Mandela became the president of South Africa in 1994. Mombaza also sang at the 1996 Olympic games in Atlanta. They've even belted out tunes on Sesame Street.

Take a trip to a rural village and you'll hear traditional black South African music. Musicians play the drums, xylophones, and flutelike instruments called *agamfes*. The high-pitched sound of whistles called *impempes* comes in short bursts throughout the music.

Kids in South Africa get involved in making music as youngsters. Black South African neighborhoods usually have at least one choir. The Soweto Songster and Kwa Thema Youth Choirs are internationally known. There is also a European-like chamber choir called the Drak-ensberg Boys Choir.

A seSotho Song

Here's a favorite children's song in seSotho, one of the many languages spoken in South Africa.

Ke Mmutlanyana	He is a furry hare
wa maboyaboya	with long ears.
wa ditsebetsebe.	
Wa re thethe.	He jumped.
Wa re potepote.	He disappeared.
Wa re dikedike!	Indeed he was gone!

Many South African tunes feature the xylophone.

41

Let's **Play!**

New playgrounds in Soweto are fun places for kids to hang out after school.

After a long week, many South African families flock to the beach for the three S's—sand, sun, and swimming. Away from the ocean, sunny South African days coax folks out to play and watch all kinds of sports. Tennis, cricket (a British game that's a little like baseball), golf, and fishing are popular, but soccer and rugby (another British game similar to American football) are the favorites.

Because soccer doesn't require expensive equipment, it's also big

Anyone up for a game of soccer? (left) **Looks like a great day to play at this beach in Durban** (below).

among South Africa's poor. In many black neighborhoods, boys and girls kick a ball around on a makeshift soccer field.

After school kids like to jump rope, play dodgeball, compete in races, and clear hurdles. Sometimes kids have fun just rolling old car tires around the neighborhood. Clever kids even bend metal scraps into toys. Some children take the metal pieces and shape them into cars. Then they attach a long handle to push them around.

Ndebele artists paint colorful geometric designs on leather bracelets and belts.

Glossary

ancestor: A relative in the past, such as a great-great-great grandparent.

continent: One of the seven great divisions of land on the globe.

desert: A dry, sandy region that receives low amounts of rainfall.

dialect: A regional variety of language that has different pronunciations from other regional varieties of the same language.

drought: A long period of dry weather, due to lack of rain or snow.

ethnic group: A large community of people that shares a number of social features in common such as language, religion, or customs.

oppression: An unfair, and sometimes harsh, use of power over a group of people.

segregated: To keep people of different ethnic groups separate, as in public schools.

veld: A grassland, usually found in southern Africa, scattered with shrubs or trees.

Look out below! This cable car runs to the top of Table Mountain, giving riders a great view of Cape Town.

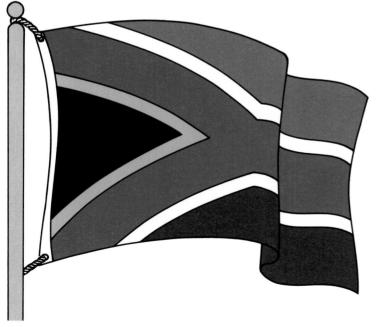

With the end of apartheid, the South African government introduced a new flag.

Pronunciation Guide

Afrikaans	ah-free-KAHNS
agamfes	ah-GUM-fehs
Agulhas	ah-GUH-lahs
apartheid	ah-PART-hate
baobab	BOW-bab
Benguela	ben-GWEH-lah
Bloemfontein	bloom-FON-tane
Boer	BOO-er
boerwors	boo-reh-VORS
braai	BREYE
impempes	im-PEMP-ehs
isicathamiya	ee-see-kah-thah-MEE-yah
Khoisan	koy-SAN
kraal	KRAWL
Kwazulu-Natal	kwah-ZOO-loo neh-TULL
Mbondgeni Ngema	um-BON-jen-ee en-GEH-mah
Ndebele	en-duh-BEH-leh
Nguni	en-GUH-nee
rikki	REE-kee
siyajabula	see-YAH-jah-BOO-lah
nifikile e	nee-fee-kay-lay AY
Sotho	SUE-too
Soweto	so-WEH-toh
Tsonga	TSON-gah
Tswana	TSWA-nah
Xhosa	KOH-zah
Zulu	ZOO-loo

Further Reading

Buettner, Dan. *Africatrek*. Minneapolis: Lerner Publications Company, 1997.

Canesso, Claudia. *South Africa*. Major World Nations series. Philadelphia: Chelsea House, 1999.

Finlayson, Reggie. *Nelson Mandela*. Minneapolis: Lerner Publications Company, 1999.

Heinrichs, Anne. A *True Book: South Africa*. New York: Children's Press, 1994.

Meisel, Jacqueline. *South Africa: A Tapestry of Peoples and Traditions*. New York: Benchmark Books, 1997.

Nabwire, Constance and Bertha Vining Montgomery. *Cooking the African Way*. Minneapolis: Lerner Publications Company, 1988.

Rosmarin, Ike. *South Africa*. Cultures of the World series. New York: Marshall Cavendish, 1993.

Ryan, Patrick. *South Africa: Facts and Places*. Child's World, Inc., 1998.

South Africa in Pictures. Minneapolis: Lerner Publications Company, 1988.

Temko, Florence. *Traditional Crafts from Africa*. Minneapolis: Lerner Publications Company, 1996.

Metric Conversion Chart

WHEN YOU KNOW:	MULTIPLY BY:	TO FIND:
teaspoon	5.0	milliliters
Tablespoon	15.0	milliliters
cup	0.24	liters
inches	2.54	centimeters
feet	0.3048	meters
miles	1.609	kilometers
square miles	2.59	square kilometers
degrees Fahrenheit	5/9 (after subtracting 32)	degrees Celsius

Index